Made in the USA
Coppell, TX
24 May 2022

78126443R00057